Paleo Slow Cooker Meals For Busy People

Emilis .B Heath

All rights reserved. Copyright © 2023 Emilis .B Heath

COPYRIGHT © 2023 Emilis .B Heath

All rights reserved.

No part of this book must be reproduced, stored in a retrieval system, or shared by any means, electronic, mechanical, photocopying, recording, or otherwise, without written permission from the publisher.

Every precaution has been taken in the preparation of this book; still the publisher and author assume no responsibility for errors or omissions. Nor do they assume any liability for damages resulting from the use of the information contained herein.

Legal Notice:

This book is copyright protected and is only meant for your individual use. You are not allowed to amend, distribute, sell, use, quote or paraphrase any of its part without the written consent of the author or publisher.

Introduction

This is a cookbook designed to cater to the dietary needs and time constraints of busy parents. The cookbook features a range of recipes that adhere to the Paleo diet, which emphasizes whole, unprocessed foods. It is divided into several sections, each offering a variety of options to suit different tastes and preferences.

In the "Beef Recipes" section, readers can find recipes that make the most of this protein source. From savory beef stews to flavorful beef roasts, these recipes offer nutritious and hearty meal options that are perfect for families.

The "Chicken Recipes" section provides a selection of recipes that feature lean and versatile chicken. Whether it's a zesty chicken curry or a comforting chicken soup, these recipes cater to a range of flavors and cooking styles.

For those who enjoy pork, the "Pork" section offers recipes that highlight the flavors of this meat. From succulent pulled pork to delectable pork chops, these dishes provide a variety of ways to enjoy pork while staying within the Paleo guidelines.

The "Others" section encompasses a range of recipes that incorporate different proteins and ingredients. From seafood dishes to turkey recipes, this section adds diversity to the cookbook and ensures there's something for everyone.

"Dessert" is the sweet finale of the cookbook, offering Paleo-friendly dessert options that can satisfy a sweet tooth without straying from the diet's principles. From fruity delights to chocolatey treats, these dessert recipes allow families to indulge in a healthier way.

This book recognizes the challenges of maintaining a Paleo diet while juggling a busy lifestyle. It provides a convenient and practical solution for parents by offering slow cooker recipes that allow for minimal hands-on cooking time. Whether you're looking to prepare a comforting family dinner or a delightful dessert, this cookbook aims to make Paleo cooking accessible and manageable for busy households.

Contents

Beef Recipes 1
  Hungry Caveman Herbed Beef Stew 1
  Ingredients 1
  Directions 1
  Back to Basics Beef Bourguignon 3
  Ingredients 3
  Directions 3
  Primordial Paprika Beef 5
  Ingredients 5
  Directions 5
  Comfort Food Saturday Night Pot Roast 7
  Ingredients 7
  Direction 7
  Paleo Pallet Pepperoncini Beef 8
  Ingredients 8
  Directions 8
  Dawn of Time Roast Beef Brisket 9
  Ingredients 9
  Directions 9
  Lactose Free Beef Stroganoff 10
  Ingredients 10
  Directions 10
  Range War Beef Pot Roast 11
  Ingredients 11
  Directions 11
  Onion Explosion Beef Bowl 12
  Ingredients 12
  Directions 12
  Paleo Chili 1 13
  Ingredients 13

- Directions 13
- Paleo Chili 2 14
  - Ingredients 14
  - Directions 14
- Ancestral Pastures Pot Roast 15
  - Ingredients 15
  - Directions 15
- Three Happiness Ginger Beef 16
  - Ingredients 16
  - Directions 16
- Mushroom Mania Real Beef Stew 17
  - Ingredients 17
  - Directions 17

Chicken Recipes 18
- Desert Dweller Chicken 18
  - Ingredients 18
  - Directions 18
- Pit Fire Spitless Chicken 19
  - Ingredients 19
  - Directions 19
- Garlicky Chicken Cacciatore 20
  - Ingredients 20
  - Directions 20
- Seven Seas Coconut Curried Bird 21
  - Ingredients 21
  - Directions 21
- India's Magic Chicken Vindaloo 22
  - Ingredients 22
  - Directions 22
- Golden Garlic Chicken 24
  - Ingredients 24
  - Directions 24
- Better Than Butter Lemon-Chicken 26

Ingredients 26
Directions 26
Tender Nibbles Garlic Wings 27
Ingredients 27
Directions 27
Nature's Treat Moroccan Stew 28
Ingredients 28
Directions 28
Salt and Spicy Thai Taste Chicken 30
Ingredients 30
Directions 30
Vitamin Infusion Paleo Soup 31
Ingredients 31
Directions 31
Campfire Classic Chicken Broth 32
Ingredients 32
Directions 32
Bits of Nature Chicken Drumsticks 33
Ingredients 33
Directions 33
Kickin' Cajun Chicken 34
Ingredients 34
Directions 34
Tasty Alternative Chicken Marsala 35
Ingredients 35
Directions 35
Fall Apart Fajitas 36
Ingredients 36
Directions 36
Earth Mother Chicken Veggie Soup 37
Ingredients 37
Directions 37
Tangy, Tasty Sweet and Sour Chicken 38

- Ingredients 38
- Directions 38
- Iron Chef Teriyaki Wings 39
- Ingredients 39
- Directions 39
- Chicken and Pork Belly Stew 40
- Ingredients 40
- Directions 40

Pork 41
- French Fields Pork Dijon 41
- Ingredients 41
- Directions 41
- Northern Steppes Sauerkraut Stew 42
- Ingredients 42
- Directions 42
- Mojave Breeze Pork 43
- Ingredients 43
- Directions 43
- Fruit and Berry Pork 44
- Ingredients 44
- Directions 44
- Proud Heritage Pork Carnitas… 45
- Ingredients 45
- Directions 45
- Stick to Your Ribs Sauerkraut and Sausage 46
- Ingredients 46
- Directions 46
- Rebel Yell Pulled Pork 47
- Ingredients 47
- Directions 47
- Earth's First Tuber Pork 48
- Ingredients 48
- Directions 48

- Oceans of Time Luau Pork 49
  - Ingredients 49
  - Directions 49
- Nature's Velvet Butternut Squash 50
  - Ingredients 50
  - Directions 50
- Wild Pickings Apple and Cranberry Pork 51
  - Ingredients 51
  - Directions 51
- Better Bacon Soup 52
  - Ingredients 52
  - Directions 52

Others 53
- Rustic Method Sweet Potato Soup 53
  - Ingredients 53
  - Directions 53
- Prehistoric Moroccan Lamb 55
  - Ingredients 55
  - Directions 55
- Mountains of Mykonos Spring Lamb 56
  - Ingredients 56
  - Directions 56
- Timeless Tilapia 57
  - Ingredients 57
  - Directions 57
- Old-Timey Shrimp Jambalaya 58
  - Ingredients 58
  - Directions 58
- Power Salmon 60
  - Ingredients 60
  - Directions 60
- Net Tossed Seafood Medley 61
  - Ingredients 61

- Directions 62
- Whole Planet Spaghetti Marinara 63
- Ingredients 63
- Directions 63
- Shoal to Shore Clam Chowder 64
- Ingredients 64
- Directions 64
- Lucky Native Turkey Soup 65
- Ingredients 65
- Directions 65
- Primordial Herb Pot Turkey 67
- Ingredients 67
- Directions 67
- Thanksgiving Forever Sweet Potatoes 68
- Ingredients 68
- Directions 68
- Bursting with Basil Chicken Minestrone 69
- Ingredients 69
- Directions 69
- Vegetable Stew 70
- Ingredients 70
- Directions 70

Dessert 72
- Day at the Country Fair Caramelized Apples 72
- Ingredients 72
- Directions 72

Beef Recipes

Hungry Caveman Herbed Beef Stew

Nothing satisfies a big hunger better than a big, hearty bowl of beef stew. For this Paleo favorite, choose a chuck roast with fat marbled throughout. The tissue and oils will melt together slowly in the crock pot to produce a tender, juicy masterpiece.

Ingredients

- 1 lb. sweet potatoes, cut into chunks
- 2 cups of carrots, cut into chunks
- 2 1/2 - 3 lbs. of beef roast
- 3 tbsp. of your favorite mustard
- 2 tsp. dried rosemary
- 2 tbsp. minced garlic
- 1 bay leaf
- 1 teaspoon sea salt
- 1/8 tsp. pepper
- 2 cups beef broth
- 1 tsp. dried thyme
- 1 medium onion, chopped

Directions

1. Mix spices and mustard.
2. Lather on beef, and place in middle of crock pot.
3. Place veggies around the outside.
4. Add beef broth.
5. Cook on low for 9 hours.

6   Discard bay leaf before serving.

Back to Basics Beef Bourguignon

French chefs traditionally use wine and pearl onions to amplify the mushroomy flavor in this: the original beef casserole. Here, sweet potatoes fill the bill, plus they add wonderful, earthy caramel notes to the broth.

Ingredients

- 3 lbs. beef sirloin, cut into 1/2" chunks
- 1/2 lbs. uncured bacon, diced
- 2 sweet potatoes, cut into chunks
- 4 carrots, diced
- 20 whole pearl onions
- 2 tbsp. minced garlic
- 1 package of your favorite mushrooms
- 1 bay leaf
- 1 tsp. sea salt
- 1/4 tsp. pepper
- 1/2 tsp. dried marjoram
- 1 tsp. thyme
- 2-3 cups of beef broth

Directions

1. Dice bacon cook in skillet over medium heat until crispy.
2. Add bacon to crock pot and discard or save lard.
3. Place beef in middle of crock pot.
4. Cut and place veggies around the outside.
5. Add spices and beef broth.

6   Cook on low for 9 hours.
7   Discard bay leaf before serving.

Primordial Paprika Beef

Chomping on a big, chewy rib bone satisfies something deep in our primitive brain. These ribs come out fork-tender, but the combination of piquant and tangy spices will make you want to keep gnawing each joint for hours.

Ingredients

- 3-4 lbs. beef short ribs
- 1 tbsp. olive oil (extra virgin preferred)
- 3 medium onions, cut into chunks
- 1 1/2 lbs. of sweet potatoes
- 1 cup carrots, cut into chunks
- 1 cup of water
- 1/2 cup red wine vinegar
- 2 tsp. dry mustard
- 2 tsp. paprika
- 2 tsp. curry
- 1 tsp. sea salt
- 1 teaspoon chili powder
- 1 tsp. arrowroot
- 1/2 tsp. pepper

Directions

1. Mix spices in separate bowl (except arrowroot).
2. Pat spices on to beef, and place in middle of crock pot.
3. Place veggies around the outside.
4. Add red wine vinegar.
5. Cook on low for 9 hours.

6   Add arrowroot after cooking. Stir and leave uncovered. Let thicken for 20 minutes.

Comfort Food Saturday Night Pot Roast

In this deceptively simple dish the marriage of onion and beef results in something more delicious altogether. Serve over a dollop of mashed roasted root vegetables as a special way to spoil yourself on a cozy night at home.

Ingredients

- 4 lbs. of beef roast
- 1 cup beef broth
- 1 large onion, diced
- 3 garlic cloves, minced
- 2 tbsp. extra virgin olive oil
- 1 bay leaf
- 1 tsp. sea salt
- 1/8 tsp. pepper

Direction

1. Coat meat with olive oil, sea salt, and pepper, and place in middle of crock pot.
2. Add garlic, bay leaf, and diced onions.
3. Add beef broth.
4. Cook on low for 9 hours.
5. Discard bay leaf before serving.

Paleo Pallet Pepperoncini Beef

Snap, spice, and tender beef: this plate's got it all. Great for work days or as a post workout treat because you can throw this hot combo together quickly in the morning and enjoy it right away as soon as you get home.

Ingredients

- 4 lbs. of beef roast
- 1 jar of pepperoncini peppers
- 1 1/2 tbsp. garlic
- 2 tbsp. Italian spices

Directions

1 Coat meat with Italian spices and garlic, and place in middle of crock pot.

2 Add pepperoncini pepper (remove stems).

3 Cook on low for 7 hours.

4 Eat with your favorite bread substitute. I prefer cabbage. Boston bib lettuce also works well.

Dawn of Time Roast Beef Brisket

The Paleo Diet evolved around a blazing fire pit. This take on brisket brings the fragrance of a campfire to the rangy - almost gamey - goodness of beef brisket.

Ingredients

- 3-4 lbs. beef brisket
- 1 tbsp. liquid smoke
- 1 tbsp. coconut oil
- 1 tbsp. garlic, minced
- 1 tbsp. sea salt
- 2 tsp. pepper

Directions

1. Coat meat with garlic, sea salt, and pepper, and place in middle of crock pot.
2. Add coconut oil and liquid smoke.
3. Cook on low for 9 hours.

Lactose Free Beef Stroganoff

We use a clever combination of coconut milk and raw honey to emulate the flavor and texture of classic stroganoff sauce, which usually comes from unhealthy sour cream. The result is so delicious you'll prefer it without starchy noodles.

Ingredients

- 2 lbs. of grass-fed ground beef
- 2 yellow onions, thinly sliced
- 1 tsp. sea salt
- 1/4 tsp. pepper
- 1 tbsp. raw honey
- 1 tbsp. your favorite mustard
- 1/2 can coconut milk (full-fat)

Directions

1. Add mustard, sea salt, pepper, and honey to pot.
2. Add in middle of crock pot. Make sure to chop up meat, so it cooks evenly.
3. Add onions.
4. Add coconut milk to crock pot, and stir it all around.
5. Cook on low for 7 hours.

Range War Beef Pot Roast

Beef is such a versatile meat. Different seasonings give it a completely different attitude. Here, centuries melt away as the flavors of carrots, celery, and onion evoke the honest goodness of Wild West chuck wagon cooking.

Ingredients

- 4 lbs. of beef roast
- 3 tbsp. extra virgin olive oil
- 1 tsp. garlic, minced
- 1 tsp. thyme
- 1 tsp. sea salt
- 1/2 tsp. dry rosemary
- 1/4 tsp. pepper
- 1 package of baby bella mushrooms, sliced
- 2 small onions, chopped
- 1/2 cup carrots, cut into chunks
- 1/2 cup celery, cut into chunks
- 2 1/2 cups beef broth
- 1 tbsp. ghee

Directions

1. Mix all spices in a separate bowl. Add mustard, sea salt, pepper, and honey to pot.
2. Rub meat with oil, and then add spices. Place meat in middle of crock pot.
3. Add all veggies around the outside of the meat.
4. Add beef broth and ghee.
5. Cook on low for 9 hours or high for 6.

Onion Explosion Beef Bowl

Cascades of fragrant, translucent onions smother hunks of robust beef in this back-to-basics classic.

Ingredients

- 4 lbs. of beef roast
- 2 tbsp. unpasteurized apple cider vinegar
- 1 tbsp. extra virgin olive oil
- 5 medium onions, sliced
- 2 cups of beef broth
- 3 1/2 tbsp. mustard
- 2 tbsp. raw honey
- 1 tsp. sea salt
- 1/4 tsp. pepper

Directions

1. Mix honey, mustard, sea salt, pepper, apple cider vinegar, and extra virgin olive oil in separate bowl.
2. Rub meat with marinade, use all of mixture. Place meat in middle of crock pot.
3. Add onions around the outside of the meat.
4. Add beef broth.
5. Cook on low for 9 hours or high for 6.

Paleo Chili 1

Traditional Southwest chili does *not* contain beans. Surprised? Once you scoop up a spoonful of this muscular, zippy beef dish loaded with cumin, you'll understand why.

Ingredients

- 2 lbs. grass-fed ground beef
- 2 cups carrots, diced
- 1 large onion, chopped
- 1 can diced tomatoes, 14oz
- 1 jar of your favorite salsa
- 1 tbsp. chili powder
- 3 tsp. cumin
- 1/8 tsp. cayenne pepper
- 1 cup beef broth
- 2 tsp. garlic, minced
- 1 tsp. sea salt
- 1/4 tsp. pepper

Directions

1. Add meat to pot and chop up with spatula. Then add all vegetables and spices.
2. Cook on low for 9 hours or high for 6.

Paleo Chili 2

Same base ingredients - entirely different flavor. For those who don't care for the Mexican herbs and spices, this "chili" version relies on paprika to give a burst of heat to the tender meat.

Ingredients

- 4 lbs. beef brisket, chopped into chunks
- 2 tbsp. ghee
- 3 medium onions, chopped
- 2 tsp. garlic
- 3 cups beef broth
- 2 cups celery, diced
- 1 tsp. dried oregano
- 1 tsp. paprika
- 1 tbsp. unpasteurized apple cider vinegar
- 1 1/8 tsp. sea salt
- 1/8 tsp. pepper

Directions

1. Add all ingredients.
2. Turn on low and cook for 9 hours.
3. Mix everything up so that the beef separates.
4. Garnish with avocado slices or a spoonful of coconut milk (full fat).

Ancestral Pastures Pot Roast

They'd been eating olives and wild garlic wild for eons. But when Ancient Europeans discovered a New World staple - the tomato - things really got cooking. As they learned, the salty olive nuggets contrast perfectly with the light tomato tang.

Ingredients

- 4 lbs. of beef roast
- 1 tsp. sea salt
- 1/8 tsp. pepper
- 1 1/2 tbsp. Italian seasoning
- 2 tsp. garlic, minced
- 1/2 cup olives, sliced
- 1 cup carrots, chopped
- 1 medium onion, sliced
- 1/2 cup beef broth
- 1/2 cup sundried tomatoes

Directions

1. Mix spices together including garlic.
2. Lather spices on beef, and place beef in center of crock pot.
3. Add carrots, onions, and sundried tomatoes around the outside of beef.
4. Add beef broth.
5. Cook on low for 9 hours or high for 6.

Three Happiness Ginger Beef

Bright notes of ginger and delicate scallions punch up this healthy Asian treat. To remain authentic, remember to choose lean meat with little fat.

Ingredients

- 3 lbs. beef stew meat
- 1/2 tsp. ground ginger
- 1 1-2 cup beef broth
- 4 tbsp. coconut aminos
- 1 tbsp. arrowroot
- 3 tbsp. coconut oil
- 1/4 cup scallions, chopped
- 4 medium onions, chopped
- 1 tbsp. garlic, minced
- 1 tsp. sea salt

Directions

1. Mix spices in separate bowl (except arrowroot).
2. Pat spices on to beef, and place in middle of crock pot.
3. Place veggies around the outside.
4. Add coconut oil, coconut aminos and beef broth.
5. Cook on low for 9 hours.
6. Add arrowroot to dish to thicken.

Mushroom Mania Real Beef Stew

Every mouthful of this dish reminds us of a deep and mysterious forest glade. The thyme helps the mushroom essence to "pop" through the dark, delicious sauce.

Ingredients

- 3 lbs. beef roast, chopped into chunks
- 1 cup beef broth
- 1/2 cup tomato paste
- 1 package cremini mushrooms, chopped
- 1 package shiitake mushrooms, chopped
- 2 cups beets, chopped
- 1/2 tsp. thyme
- 1/2 tsp. dry rosemary
- 1 tbsp. garlic, minced
- 1 teaspoon sea salt
- 1/2 teaspoon pepper
- 2 tbsp. olive oil

Directions

1. Mix rosemary, thyme, sea salt, and pepper in a separate bowl.
2. Pat spices on to beef, and place in middle of crock pot.
3. Place veggies around the outside.
4. Mix garlic, beef broth, and tomato paste. Add to crock pot.
5. Cook on low for 9 hours.

Chicken Recipes

Desert Dweller Chicken

The key to this dish is cilantro: bold, fresh, and as surprising as a desert sunrise. Although we think of cilantro as the key Southwest spice, it originally grew wild in Europe, Asia, and Africa where our ancestors must have loved it as much as we do.

Ingredients

- 3 lbs. boneless free range chicken thighs, chopped into chunks
- 3 cups of sweet potatoes, chopped into chunks
- 2 medium onions, chopped into chunks
- 1 can diced tomatoes, 14oz
- 1 jar of your favorite salsa (I like Jack's Special)
- 2 tsp. cumin
- 1 tsp. paprika
- 1/8 tsp. cayenne
- 1 tbsp. cilantro
- 1 tsp. oregano
- 1 tsp. sea salt
- 1/4 tsp. pepper

Directions

1. Add all ingredients to the crock pot.
2. Gently mix all ingredients.
3. Cook on low for 8 hours.

Pit Fire Spitless Chicken

Imagine crouching around a fire pit slowly turning a bird stuffed with rosemary and herbs on a spit over the flames. Is your mouth watering yet? It will be when you taste the easy, convenient modern dish that embodies all the same flavors.

Ingredients

- 2-3 lbs. whole free range chicken
- 1 tbsp. garlic, minced
- 1 onion, chopped
- 1 tsp. thyme
- 1 tsp. rosemary
- 1 tsp. sea salt
- 1/4 tsp. pepper
- 2 cups free range chicken broth

Directions

1. Wash and dry chicken.
2. Add spices to chicken.
3. Crumble up four small two-inch balls of aluminum foil (to keep chicken propped up).
4. Then add chicken to crock pot.
5. Add onion over top of chicken.
6. Pour chicken broth over top.
7. Cook on low for 9 hours or on high for 5.

Garlicky Chicken Cacciatore

For millions of years native Europeans, Africans, and Asians reaped the benefits of the delicious, pungent super food: garlic. This take on an Italian classic bursts with tangy, heart-healthy garlicky goodness.

Ingredients

- 3 lbs. boneless free range chicken breasts
- 1 jar of your favorite tomato sauce
- 1 package white mushrooms, sliced
- 1 tbsp. garlic
- 2 medium onions, sliced
- 1 1/2 tsp. sea salt
- 1.2 tsp. pepper
- 1 red pepper, sliced
- 1/2 tsp. oregano
- 1/2 tsp. basil
- 2 tbsp. extra virgin olive oil

Directions

1. Add app ingredients to crock pot.
2. Cook on low for 9 hours.
3. Serve with rice pasta (if you are okay with "safe starches"), or garlic cauliflower "rice".

Seven Seas Coconut Curried Bird

Silky coconut-milk laced with fiery curry support the raw energy of Paleo protein in this Pacific -Island inspired hotpot. Feel free to adjust the seasoning to suit your untamed taste.

Ingredients

- 3 lbs. boneless free range chicken breasts, chopped into chunks
- 3 tbsp. ghee
- 2 medium onions, sliced
- 1 can of coconut milk (full fat), 14oz
- 1 tsp. sea salt
- 1/8 tsp. pepper
- 2 tbsp. curry
- 1 cup free range chicken broth
- 1/4 cup dried coconut flakes
- 2 tsp. garlic, minced
- 1 tbsp. ginger
- 1 tsp. chili powder

Directions

1. Mix coconut milk, spices, and free range chicken broth, then add to crock pot.
2. Add meat and veggies.
3. Cook on low for 7 hours.
4. Add coconut flakes before serving.

India's Magic Chicken Vindaloo

The tradition of toasting zesty coriander and mustard seeds over a blazing fire goes back so far, no one can pinpoint exactly when it began. The idea was to unleash the deepest flavor of the seed blend. Here, we achieve the same exotic Indian style with long, slow crock pot cooking.

Ingredients

- 3 lbs. boneless skinless free range chicken breast, cut into chunks
- 4 tbsp. curry powder
- 2 tsp. garlic, minced
- 2 tbsp. ginger
- 3 tbsp. extra virgin olive oil
- 1/2 tsp. paprika
- 1/2 tsp. ground cumin
- 1/2 tsp. ground coriander
- 2 tsp. mustard seeds
- 1/8 tsp. cayenne pepper
- 1/4 cup white wine vinegar
- 1/4 cup tomato paste
- 1 medium onions, sliced
- 1 cup tomatoes, diced
- 1 tbsp. cumin
- 1 tsp. turmeric

Directions

1. Mix spices and tomato paste, olive oil, and vinegar, then add to crock pot.

2   Add meat and veggies.
3   Cook on low for 6 hours.

Golden Garlic Chicken

The scent of sage and rosemary reminds everyone of great feast day celebrations: Thanksgiving, Christmas, and New Year's. Thanks to this juicy, aromatic recipe, every day is a time to celebrate.

Ingredients

- 2-3 lbs. whole free range chicken
- 3 tbsp. ghee
- 1 medium onion, sliced
- 1 1/2 cups free range chicken broth
- 4 tbsp. garlic, minced
- 1 tsp. rosemary
- 1/2 tsp. oregano
- 1/2 tsp. sage
- 1/2 tsp. thyme
- 1 tsp. sea salt
- 1/2 tsp. pepper

Directions

1. Wash and dry chicken.
2. Rub chicken with ghee.
3. Add spices to chicken.
4. Crumble up four small two-inch balls of aluminum foil (to keep chicken propped up).
5. Add chicken to crock pot.
6. Add onion on top of the chicken.
7. Pour chicken broth over top.

8   Cook on low for 9 hours or on high for 5.

Better Than Butter Lemon-Chicken

Missing the rich, sweet melding that butter mixed with lemon can lend to dips and sauces? This recipe recaptures that perfect pairing while removing the unhealthy lactose proteins.

Ingredients

- 2-3 lbs. whole free range chicken
- 3 tbsp. ghee
- 1 tsp. rosemary
- 1/2 tsp. thyme
- 2 tsp. garlic, minced
- 1/2 cup free range chicken broth
- 1 tsp. sea salt
- 1/8 tsp. pepper
- 1/4 cup lemon juice
- 1/2 tsp. onion powder

Directions

1. Wash and dry chicken.
2. Rub chicken with ghee.
3. Add spices to chicken.
4. Crumble up four small two-inch balls of aluminum foil (to keep chicken propped up).
5. Add chicken to crock pot.
6. Pour chicken broth and lemon over the top.
7. Cook on low for 9 hours or on high for 5.

Tender Nibbles Garlic Wings

Funny thing about garlic: When you cook it long enough it mellows and turns savory, retaining just enough kick to keep it interesting. It's a perfect complement for fatty, delicate chicken wings. Serve this recipe as a portable snack for a game day, tailgating, or backyard outing.

Ingredients

- 3 lbs. free range chicken wings
- 3 tbsp. garlic, minced
- 3 tbsp. coconut oil
- 1 tsp. sea salt
- 1/2 tsp. pepper
- 1/2 cup free range chicken broth
- 1/8 tsp. cayenne pepper
- 1 tsp. rosemary

Directions

1. Mix all ingredients (except chicken wings and broth) in separate bowl.
2. Toss wings in mixture and transfer to crock pot.
3. Add chicken broth over top of wings.
4. Cook on low for 7 hours.

Nature's Treat Moroccan Stew

Wild grapes - those that escape the birds - hang on the vine in the autumn sunshine dries and sweetens them into raisins: nature's first snack food. Like our Moroccan ancestors, we use them to add bright notes to a hearty stew.

Ingredients

- 3 lbs. boneless skinless free range chicken breasts, chopped into chunks
- 1 cup free range chicken stock
- 1 tbsp. arrowroot
- 2 tsp. garlic, minced
- 1 zucchini sliced
- 1/4 cup raisins
- 2 tsp. ginger
- 1 tsp. cumin
- 1 tsp. cinnamon
- 1/2 tsp. paprika
- 1/4 tsp. cayenne pepper
- 1 tsp. sea salt
- 1/2 tsp. pepper
- 1/4 cup tomato paste
- 3 medium onions, chopped
- 1/3 cup almonds, slivered

Directions

1. Add tomato paste, chicken stock, and raisins to crock pot.
2. Mix spices and garlic in separate bowl.

3   Toss chicken in mixture. Place everything in crock pot.

4   Stir in all veggies.

5   Cook on low for 9 hours.

6   Add arrowroot after cooking. Stir and leave uncovered. Let thicken for 20 minutes.

7   Garnish with slivered almonds.

Salt and Spicy Thai Taste Chicken

Sharp hints of lime cut across, crisp zest of onions and nutty, salty cashew nuggets in this authentic Asian classic. Every bite offers a taste of Ancient Siam.

Ingredients

- 3 lbs. free range chicken thighs
- 3 green onions, sliced
- 1/4 cup cashew butter
- 1 half can of coconut milk (full fat)
- 1 half lime squeezed
- 1 1/2 tbsp. coconut aminos
- 2 tsp. ginger
- 1/4 cup cashews, chopped
- 1/8 tsp. cayenne pepper
- 1 medium onion, chopped
- 1 tbsp. cilantro
- 1 tsp. sea salt
- 1/8 tsp. pepper

Directions

1. Add all ingredients except for cashews.
2. Cook on low for 9 hours.
3. Use chopped cashews for garnish. Cilantro also works well.

Vitamin Infusion Paleo Soup

Poor, underappreciated cabbage: Hardy, healthy, full of vitamin C, and bursting with raw power. It's fallen out of favor in modern cooking. Here we take a tip from our bronze-age ancestors and cook the cabbage until it loses it's bitter edge resulting in velvety mild leaves that give off a fragrant perfume.

Ingredients

- 3 lbs. boneless skinless free range chicken breasts, sliced
- 5 cups of free range chicken broth
- 3 cups carrots, chopped
- 1 tbsp. garlic
- 2 cups celery, chopped
- 2 cups green cabbage, sliced
- 2 medium onions, sliced
- 1 tsp. sea salt
- 1/8 tsp. pepper
- 1/2 tsp. oregano
- 1/2 tsp. rosemary
- 1/2 tsp. thyme
- 1 bay leaf
- 1/4 cup green onions, chopped
- 1 tbsp. parsley

Directions

1. Add all ingredients.
2. Cook on low for 8 hours.
3. Discard bay leaf before serving.

Campfire Classic Chicken Broth

Ancient people around the world discovered that if they threw meat, vegetables, and scraps together into a pot and cooked them long and slow over the fire, the result was a delicious, healthy broth. Here we use that tried-and-true method to capture the primitive essence of good taste. Use this broth as a soup base or add to other stew recipes for a double shot of protein.

Ingredients

- 2-3 lbs. leftover free range chicken carcass
- 3 stalks celery, sliced down middle
- 2 medium onions, quartered
- 2 medium carrots, cut in chunks
- 1 sprig fresh parsley (or 1 tsp. dried)
- 6 cups water
- 2 tsp. sea salt
- 1 tsp. pepper

Directions

1. Place chicken in the middle of crock pot.
2. Add water, spices, and vegetables.
3. Cook on low for 7 hours.

Bits of Nature Chicken Drumsticks

Joints of a bird, a handful of mushrooms, and a dollop of honey: this Paleo meal-in-a-pot truly brings the ingredients from a day of wilderness hunting and foraging into a modern kitchen.

Ingredients

- 3 lbs. free range chicken drumsticks
- 2 tbsp. coconut amino acids
- 1 package of mushrooms, sliced
- 1 onion, sliced
- 2 tbsp. raw honey
- 1 tsp. garlic, minced
- 1 cup jarred tomato sauce

Directions

1. Mix tomato sauce, garlic, honey, and coconut aminos in a separate bowl.
2. Toss drumsticks in mixture and transfer to crock pot.
3. Add mushrooms and onions.
4. Cook on low for 8 hours.

Kickin' Cajun Chicken

Deep in the heart of the bayou, they like their food the way they like their music: spicy, hot, and bursting with Creole energy. This recipe brings the brightest North American and Old World natural flavors together in a dish that will make you want to kick up your heels.

Ingredients

- 3 lbs. boneless skinless free range chicken thighs
- 1 can diced tomatoes, 14oz
- 1/2 cup onion, chopped
- 1/4 cup celery, chopped
- 1/2 cup red or green pepper
- 2 tsp. garlic, minced
- 1 tsp. sea salt
- 1/2 tsp. pepper
- 1 tsp. paprika
- 1/8 tsp. cayenne pepper

Directions

1. Mix all spices together.
2. Rub spices into meat, and add to crock pot.
3. Add vegetables (tomatoes, pepper, onion, and celery).
4. Cook on low for 9 hours.

Tasty Alternative Chicken Marsala

In the traditional version of this Italian favorite sweet marsala, wine is reduced down to a sauce that veils mushrooms and thin fillets of pressed veal or chicken. Here we've found a way to lock in that sweet meat and mushroom combo using olive oil and ghee. *Mangia bene!* (Eat well!)

Ingredients

- 3 lbs. boneless skinless free range chicken breasts
- 1 tsp. garlic, minced
- 1 tbsp. olive oil
- 2 tbsp. ghee
- 1 tsp. sea salt
- 1/2 tsp. pepper
- 1/2 tsp. oregano
- 1 package baby bella mushrooms, sliced
- 1 cup free range chicken broth
- 1 1/2 parsley

Directions

1. Mix all dry spices.
2. Pat spices onto dried chicken breasts, then add to crock pot.
3. Add chicken broth, ghee and garlic.
4. Add mushrooms.
5. Cook for 6 hours.
6. If sauce isn't thick to your liking, remove lid and let it simmer for 20 minutes.
7. Garnish with chives.

Fall Apart Fajitas

Don't you love the aroma that rises when highly seasoned meat first hits the sizzling surface of a fajita grill? This recipe captures that essence with almost no effort on your part. The long cook method softens the chicken and infuses it with the Mexican flavors you love. Remember the longer a spice cooks the brighter it gets, so if you're worried about the dish becoming too hot decrease the amount of chili powder you use.

Ingredients

- 3 lbs. boneless skinless free range chicken breasts
- 1 jar of your favorite salsa
- 2 tbsp. chili powder
- 1 tablespoon ground cumin
- 2 teaspoons kosher sea salt
- 1 tsp. pepper
- 2 teaspoons paprika
- 1 teaspoon ground coriander
- 1/2 teaspoon cayenne pepper
- 1 lime, juiced
- 2 tbsp. fresh cilantro

Directions

1. Add salsa, dry seasonings, and lime juice to crock pot.
2. Add chicken breasts. Cover breasts with salsa.
3. Cook on low for 7 hours.
4. Take two forks and shred the chicken before serving.

Earth Mother Chicken Veggie Soup

After decades of study, scientists have finally concluded that chicken soup actually *can* help cure the common cold - just as hundreds of millions of mothers around the world discovered long ago. The broth hydrates cells and boosts immune response; the vegetables infuse the soup with vitamins: a win-win-win that's simply delicious. But don't wait until you're sick to try it. This soup makes a wonderful, light summer dinner or a hearty winter lunch.

Ingredients

- 3 lbs. boneless skinless free range chicken thighs
- 2 cup carrots, chopped
- 1 package of mushrooms, sliced
- 1 small onion, chopped
- 1 zucchini, chopped
- 1/4 cup celery, chopped
- 4 cups of free range chicken broth
- 1 can diced tomatoes, 14oz
- 1 tsp. sea salt
- 1/4 tsp. pepper
- 1 tbsp. basil
- 1/4 tsp. oregano

Directions

1. Add all ingredients to crock pot.
2. Cook on low for 6 hours.

Tangy, Tasty Sweet and Sour Chicken

The fabulous secret about pineapple is that it serves as a natural meat tenderizer. This means each sweet and juicy morsel does double duty, imparting a tangy oriental flavor and breaking down meat fibers so that the chicken becomes easy to digest and melt in your mouth.

Ingredients

- 3 lbs. boneless skinless free range chicken breasts, cut into chunks
- 2 cups of pineapple, cut into chunks
- 1 cup carrots, cut into chunks
- 1 medium onion, chopped
- 2 red peppers, sliced
- 3 tbsp. raw honey
- 1/3 cup coconut aminos
- 1 tsp. ginger
- 1 tsp. garlic, minced
- 1/4 cup free range chicken stock
- 1 tsp. arrowroot
- 1 tsp. sea salt

Directions

1. Add all ingredients (except arrowroot) to crock pot.
2. Mix to coat chicken evenly.
3. Cook on low for 7 hours.
4. Add arrowroot after cooking. Stir and leave uncovered. Let thicken for 20 minutes.

Iron Chef Teriyaki Wings

Japanese cooks are masters of simplicity. They really know how to bring out the essence of a wild-caught fish, a raw vegetable, or a protein by preparing it with a basic sauce that won't distract from the primary ingredients' taste. No doubt this uncomplicated approach is why teriyaki has become an international favorite. We step back to basics in our version, substituting raw honey and coconut oil for over-processed soy sauce.

Ingredients

- 3 lbs. free range chicken wings
- 2 tbsp. raw honey
- 1 tsp. garlic, minced
- 1 tsp. ginger
- 1/2 cup coconut aminos
- 1/2 cup water
- 1/2 cup pineapple, diced
- 1/4 cup coconut oil
- 1/8 tsp. cayenne pepper

Directions

1. Mix all ingredients (except chicken wings) in separate bowl.
2. Toss wings in mixture and transfer to crock pot.
3. Add the rest of the mixture over top of the wings.
4. Cook on low for 7 hours.

Chicken and Pork Belly Stew

The mingling of two meats - say, wild boar and wild birds - must be a very ancient flavor, since Paleo hunters would throw everything they caught onto the fire together. This recipe offers you that primordial taste sensation in an easy modern form. The pork renders slowly, coating the chicken in a jacket of protective, rendered fat. Simply delicious!

Ingredients

- 3 lbs. free range chicken breast, sliced
- 1/2 lbs. uncured bacon
- 1 medium onion, sliced
- 2 medium carrots, chopped
- 2 cups free range chicken broth
- 1/2 cup coconut milk
- 1 tsp. sea salt
- 1/8 tsp. pepper
- 1/2 tsp. oregano

Directions

1. Cook bacon in skillet over medium heat until crispy.
2. Discard or save lard and transfer bacon to cutting board.
3. Dice the bacon and toss into the crockpot.
4. Add chicken breasts.
5. Add coconut milk, chicken broth, sea salt, and pepper.
6. Add carrots and onions.
7. Cook on high for 7 hours.

Pork

French Fields Pork Dijon

Every mouthful of this luscious dish will burst over your tongue like the yellow blooms of wild mustard across the fields of old France. Meaty cremini mushrooms - the baby version of portobellos - act like little sponges, soaking up the tangy pork juices and delivering them directly to your taste buds.

Ingredients

- 3 lbs. pork shoulder
- 2 cups vegetable broth
- 2 medium onions, sliced
- 1 package of cremini mushrooms, sliced
- 1/4 cup Dijon mustard
- 1 tbsp. rosemary
- 1 tsp. sea salt
- 1/2 tsp. black pepper

Directions

1. Rub pork shoulder with Dijon mustard and add to middle of crock pot.
2. Add vegetable broth.
3. Add mushrooms, onions on top and around the outside.
4. Cook on low for 9 hours.

Northern Steppes Sauerkraut Stew

In the harsh, cold climates of the north, peasants learned that salted, stored cabbage would change into something miraculous over the months: sauerkraut. Make this dish and you'll discover another amazing transformation. When simmered, the acidic vinegar strings of kraut change to sweet, fragrant shreds of apple-scented delight.

Ingredients

- 3 lbs. pork roast, cut into chunks
- 1 jar of your favorite sauerkraut (I'm a huge fan of Bubbies)
- 1 cup vegetable broth
- 1 apple peeled, cored, and diced
- 2 tsp. garlic
- 1/2 tsp. rosemary
- 1 medium onion, sliced
- 1/2 tsp. dill
- 1 tbsp. your favorite mustard
- 1 tsp. sea salt
- 1 tsp. caraway seeds
- 1/8 tsp. pepper

Directions

1. Add all ingredients to the crock pot.
2. Cook on low for 7 hours.

Mojave Breeze Pork

While this dish is cooking, open the crop pot lid just a crack and you'll get a whiff not only of garlic, but of authentic Mojave desert freshness. That's the smell of sage and rosemary which grow in mass profusion throughout the southland desert. We find that because of its mild taste, the pork in this composition is a perfect vehicle for the herbs.

Ingredients

- 3 lbs. pork roast
- 2 tbsp. coconut oil
- 2 medium onions, chopped
- 1 tbsp. garlic, minced
- 1 tsp. sea salt
- 1/2 tsp. pepper
- 1 cup vegetable broth
- 1 tsp. sage
- 2 tsp. rosemary
- 1/2 tsp. oregano

Directions

1. Mix all dry spices in separate bowl.
2. Pat spices onto pork and add to crock pot.
3. Add vegetable broth, garlic, onions and coconut oil.
4. Cook on low for 8 hours.

Fruit and Berry Pork

Should we call this a main course, or special occasion dessert? Sweet, spicy, Christmassy flavors of cranberry and orange unfurl with every luscious bite. It's the perfect way to serve up a fancy feast for holidays, but easy enough to whip up any time.

Ingredients

- 3 lbs. pork roast, cut into chunks
- 1 tsp. orange zest
- 1/4 cup vegetable broth
- 1 tsp. sea salt
- 1/8 tsp. pepper
- 1 medium onion, chopped
- 1 tsp. garlic, minced
- 1 granny smith peeled, cored, and diced
- 1/4 cup of cranberries
- 1 tsp. raw honey
- 1/4 cup green onions, sliced
- 1/4 tsp. paprika
- 1/4 tsp. allspice
- 1/2 tsp. ginger

Directions

1. Add app ingredients to crock pot.
2. Stir to make sure everything is coated evenly.
3. Cook on low for 7 hours.
4. If sauce has not thickened, remove the lid and let simmer for 20 minutes.

Proud Heritage Pork Carnitas…

Long and slow – that's the secret to cooking authentic Mexican carnitas. For this fiesta-in-your-mouth we start with a chipotle, oregano and cumin rub that sinks deep into shreds of succulent pork. It's so good you'll be glad to skip tradition and eat it by the forkful without the tortilla.

Ingredients

- 3 lbs. pork shoulder
- 1 tbsp. garlic, minced
- 3 tbsp. coconut oil
- 1 medium onion, chopped
- 1 tsp. cumin
- 1 tsp. oregano
- 1/2 tsp. paprika
- 1 tsp. sea salt
- 1/4 tsp. pepper
- 1/8 tsp. cayenne pepper
- 1 tsp. chipotle pepper (or chili pepper)
- Avocado and fresh cilantro for garnish

Directions

1. Mix all dry spices, garlic and coconut oil.
2. Rub spices into pork shoulder and place in middle of the crock pot.
3. Add the rest of the ingredients.
4. Cook on low for 8 hours.
5. Use two forks to shred pork before serving.
6. Garnish with avocado slices and cilantro.

Stick to Your Ribs Sauerkraut and Sausage

The magic ingredient to this yummy concoction is kielbasa, a simple pork sausage forever linked with Poland. What makes kielbasa so special? Because a single ingredient, marjoram, provides its unique flavor. Hearty hunks of pork balance out this deceptively simple meal.

Ingredients

- 2 lbs. pork roast, cut into chunks
- 1 lbs. kielbasa sausage, cut into chunks
- 2 tbsp. coconut oil
- 1 teaspoon dried thyme
- 1/2 teaspoon ground mustard
- 1/2 teaspoon dried oregano
- 1 teaspoon sea salt
- 1/4 teaspoon pepper
- 1 tbsp. raw honey
- 1 jar of your favorite sauerkraut

Directions

1. Add all ingredients to crock pot.
2. Mix around to ensure an even coating.
3. Cook low for 8 hours.

Rebel Yell Pulled Pork

Tangy, juicy and ready to eat alone or heaped on your favorite root veggies, pulled pork is an American classic. We love the sweet and tart dance that occurs between the pungent cider and syrupy raw honey.

Ingredients

- 3 lbs. pork roast
- 1 tsp. sea salt
- 1/2 tsp. pepper
- 1 medium onion, chopped
- 2 tsp. garlic, minced
- 1 cup beef broth
- 1 tbsp. unpasteurized apple cider vinegar
- 1 tbsp. raw honey
- 3 tablespoons paprika
- 1 tablespoon dry mustard
- 1/2 tsp. cayenne

Directions

1. Mix dry spices, garlic, honey and apple cider vinegar together in separate bowl.
2. Pat into dry pork roast and add to center of crock pot.
3. Add beef broth and onion.
4. Cook on low for 7 hours.
5. Use two forks to pull apart the pork.

Earth's First Tuber Pork

Unlike the cultivated white potato which is highly glycemic, the sweet potato is a natural tuber root loaded with vitamin C, A and soluble fiber. Better yet, it blends with pork fat to impart a caramel-like sweetness to the entire dish.

Ingredients

- 3 lbs. pork roast, chopped into chunks
- 1 tbsp. olive oil
- 1 tsp. sea salt
- 1/2 tsp. pepper
- 3 sweet potatoes, chopped into chunks
- 1 medium onion, sliced
- 1 tbsp. garlic, minced
- 1 cup free range chicken broth
- 1/2 tsp. rosemary
- 1/4 tsp. thyme
- 3 tbsp. Dijon mustard

Directions

1. Add all ingredients to crock pot.
2. Mix all ingredients to ensure an even coating.
3. Cook on low for 8 hours.

Oceans of Time Luau Pork

The origin of ham, like jerky, is lost in prehistory. If you shop wisely, you are likely to find one made the traditional way - with no additives other than salt and smoke. If even this amount of modernity is too much for you, do as our Hawaiian ancestors did and toss a shoulder of pork in the mix as a substitute. Either way, the result will overflow with South Sea Island flavor.

Ingredients

- 3 lbs. bone in ham
- 2 cups pineapple, diced
- 1/4 tsp. pepper
- 1 tbsp. raw honey
- 2 tbsp. unpasteurized apple cider vinegar
- 1 tsp. ground cloves
- 1 tbsp. coconut oil

Directions

1. Rub coconut oil on bottom of crock pot.
2. Add ham to middle of crock pot.
3. Mix honey, pineapples, cloves and pepper.
4. Spread mixture over top of pork.
5. Cook on low for 6 to 8 hours.

Nature's Velvet Butternut Squash

Whoever named this vegetable had it right. Butternut squash does indeed impart a buttery flavor and creamy mouth feel to any meal, but especially when prepared like this. We capitalize on the similarity to dairy butter by adding ghee to the stew, but feel free to substitute olive oil if that's your preference.

Ingredients

- 3 lbs. pork roast, cut into chunks
- 2 cups carrots, chopped
- 1 medium onion, chopped
- 2 cups butternut squash, chopped
- 1 cup free range chicken broth
- 1 tsp. sage
- 1 tsp. thyme
- 1 tsp. sea salt
- 1/2 tsp. pepper
- 3 tbsp. ghee
- 1 bay leaf
- 1/2 tsp. rosemary

Directions

1. Add all ingredients to crock pot.
2. Mix to ensure an even coating.
3. Cook on low for 7 hours.
4. Discard bay leaf before serving.

Wild Pickings Apple and Cranberry Pork

Something from the bog (cranberries), something from the trees (apples), and something from the meadows (pork): This dish falls together like a hunter-gatherer's dream. Add a dash of cinnamon, and you have a meal perfect for fall and winter special occasions.

Ingredients

- 3 lbs. pork roast
- 3 tbsp. raw honey
- 2 tbsp. unpasteurized apple cider vinegar
- 1 tsp. sea salt
- 1/4 tsp. pepper
- 1 tsp. ginger
- 1/2 tsp. cinnamon
- 1/4 cup dried cranberries
- 2 tart apples, peeled, cored, and diced
- 1 tbsp. coconut oil

Directions

1. Mix all dried spices, honey, apple cider vinegar and coconut oil.
2. Spread mixture over dry pork; add pork to middle of crock pot.
3. Add rest of mixture over top of pork.
4. Add apples and cranberries over top.
5. Cook on low for 8 hours.

Better Bacon Soup

Crave dairy no more! We've carefully crafted a replacement that offers the same creamy satisfaction as dairy using coconut milk, vegetable broth and spices. Uncured bacon, cooked slowly, renders down into the salty, savory accents so many of us have come to associate with cured bacon. Comfort food at its best!

Ingredients

- 1 lbs. uncured bacon, minced
- 6 cups vegetable broth
- 1 can of coconut milk (full fat), 14oz
- 2 cups carrots, chopped
- 1 medium onion, chopped
- 1/2 cup celery, chopped
- 1 tsp. sea salt
- 1/2 tsp. pepper
- 1 tsp. sage
- 2 tsp. rosemary
- 1/2 tsp. oregano

Directions

1. Cook bacon in skillet over medium heat until crispy.
2. Add lard to crockpot and transfer bacon to cutting board.
3. Dice the bacon and toss into the crockpot.
4. Add all other ingredients to crock pot.
5. Cook on low for 5 hours.

Others

Rustic Method Sweet Potato Soup

Our Paleo forbearers must have been thrilled when they saw how fire turned tough knotty roots into tender victuals. With another tip of our hat to ancient wisdom, we use our "electric fire" to turn fibrous turnips and sweet potatoes into satisfyingly smooth and ultra-healthy soup. Notice the hint of nutmeg? It's a little inspiration from the classic French cuisine.

Ingredients

- 4 sweet potatoes, cut into small chunks
- 1 turnip, chopped
- 1/2 cup coconut milk
- 6 cups free range chicken broth
- 1 tbsp. raw honey
- 1 tsp. nutmeg
- 2 tbsp. ghee
- 1 tsp. sea salt
- 1/8 tsp. pepper
- 1 medium onion, chopped
- 1 cinnamon stick
- 1/4 tsp. ginger

Directions

1. Add all ingredients to crock pot.
2. Gently stir all ingredients.
3. Cook on low for 7 hours.

4   Discard cinnamon stick before serving.

Prehistoric Moroccan Lamb

In Morocco they've probably been eating wild ungulates (sheep or goats) since at least 200,000 B.C. when humans first arrived there. Obviously, they've had plenty of time to "get it right!" We take their cue and incorporate the rich heritage of Moroccan local spices into our crock pot version of this lamb dish. Note: When preparing lamb chops, trim away excess fat (sometimes called "fell") to avoid gaminess - unless you prefer an untamed taste.

Ingredients

- 2 lbs. lamb chops
- 1 medium onion, diced
- 1 tbsp. coconut oil
- 1 tbsp. cumin
- 2 tsp. garlic minced
- 2 tsp. paprika
- 1 tsp. turmeric
- 1/2 tsp. cinnamon
- 1 tsp. sea salt
- 1/4 tsp. pepper

Directions

1. Place onion in a crock pot.
2. Mix all dry spices and coconut oil.
3. Rub over lamb chops and toss in crock pot.
4. Add onions and garlic over top.
5. Cook on low for 5 hours.

Mountains of Mykonos Spring Lamb

Americans don't eat as much lamb as other carnivores the world over. Too bad! Lamb is not only massively healthy; it's especially easy to digest too. Mint adds a zesty freshness to this Greek style spring lamb feast.

Ingredients

- 3 lbs. leg of lamb, bone-in
- 3 tbsp. ghee
- 1 tbsp. garlic, minced
- 1 tsp. oregano
- 2 tsp. nutmeg
- 1 tsp. mint
- 1 tsp. sea salt
- 1/4 pepper
- 2 tsp. raw honey
- 1 medium lemon, juiced
- 1 cup scallions, sliced
- 1 tbsp. coconut oil

Directions

1. Rub coconut oil along bottom of crock pot.
2. Mix all ingredients except lamb and scallions.
3. Rub mixture over lamb and place in middle of crock pot.
4. Add sliced scallions over top of lamb.
5. Cook on low for 9 hours.

Timeless Tilapia

Tilapia fish has been a human staple for so long; it actually has its own ancient Egyptian hieroglyph! Finally, we in the west are discovering its firm, delicate flesh and light flavor. We think lemon is much better than heavy butter or breading at bringing the essence of this unassuming river species. The bright flavor of dill provides a sprightly note to the meal.

Ingredients

- 2 lbs. Tilapia (halibut works as well)
- 2 tbsp. extra virgin olive oil
- 1 large tomato, chopped
- 1 tbsp. parsley
- 1/2 medium lemon, juiced
- 1/2 tsp. sea salt
- 1 tsp. pepper
- 1 tsp. garlic
- 1 tsp. dill

Directions

1. Spread one tbsp. olive oil to bottom of crock pot.
2. Mix dry spices, garlic, and second tbsp. of olive oil.
3. Rub over fish and add to middle of the crock pot.
4. Squeeze lemon over top.
5. Add chopped tomato.
6. Cook on low for 2 hours.

Old-Timey Shrimp Jambalaya

The scent of the sea, the snap of peppers, and the crunch of celery: these are the organic ingredients that identify a truly great Louisiana Jambalaya. Here we rely on the ages-old Louisiana spice combo to bring an ocean of flavor to your mouth.

Ingredients

- 1 lbs. wild caught shrimp, deveined and shelled
- 1 lbs. sausage, chopped
- 1/4 cup tomato paste
- 1 can diced tomatoes, 14oz
- 1 can vegetable broth, 14oz
- 2 tbsp. ghee
- 2 medium onions, chopped
- 1/2 cup celery, chopped
- 1 tbsp. garlic, minced
- 2 red peppers, sliced
- 2 tbsp. paprika
- 1 tbsp. ground cumin
- 1/4 tsp. cayenne
- 1 tsp. sea salt
- 1/2 tsp. pepper

Directions

1. Add all ingredients except shrimp.
2. Mix to ensure an even coating.
3. Cook on low for 5 hours.

4   Add shrimp and cook for 25 more minutes (make sure shrimp is pink).

Power Salmon

Salmon grow muscular and flavorful as they traverse the oceans and fresh waters of the world. Thus, it's one of the few fishes sturdy enough to hold up to a long slow cooking and oily enough to pair well with acidic citrus juices. This dish capitalizes on that robustness with a simple squirt of lime and a handful of cilantro dressing.

Ingredients

- 2 lbs. wild-caught salmon, thawed
- 1 tsp. garlic, minced
- 2 tbsp. raw honey
- 1 lime, juiced
- 1 tbsp. cilantro
- 1 tsp. chipotle pepper (or chili powder)
- 1 tbsp. coconut aminos

Directions

1. Mix all ingredients in separate dish.
2. Rub onto salmon and place in middle of crock pot.
3. Add the rest of mixture over top of salmon.
4. Cook on low for 2 hours.

Net Tossed Seafood Medley

In this recipe a ménage of seafood cook together as one. The strong blend of ocean tastes harkens back to the days when our ancestors would eagerly gobble down anything and everything their nets brought in. The juices of each fish leach out and mingle to form a glistening, delicious, slightly saline broth enhanced by the tomatoes.

Ingredients

- 1 lbs. cod or haddock
- 1 lbs. wild-caught shrimp
- 1 can crabmeat (6-8oz)
- 1 can chopped clams (6-8oz)
- 1 can diced tomatoes
- 1 can tomato paste (6oz)
- 2 medium onions, chopped
- 1/2 cup carrots, chopped
- 1/2 cup celery
- 1 tbsp. garlic, minced
- 1/2 cup vegetable broth
- 1 tbsp. olive oil
- 1 tsp. paprika
- 1/8 tsp. cayenne pepper
- 1 tbsp. parsley
- 1 bay leaf
- 2 teaspoons dried basil
- 1 teaspoon dried oregano
- 1 teaspoon dried thyme

- 1 tsp. sea salt
- 1/2 tsp. pepper

Directions

1. Add all ingredients except shrimp.
2. Mix to ensure an even coating.
3. Cook on low for 3 hours.
4. Add shrimp and cook for 25 more minutes (make sure shrimp is pink).
5. Discard bay leaf before eating.

Whole Planet Spaghetti Marinara

Who needs processed stands of wheat gluten when the earth has given us the spaghetti squash? This is one shrimp marinara that will leave you feeling satisfied, but not stuffed. Our much more flavorful alternative Italian dish replaces goopy red sauce with a light, fresh, tomato foundation. Perfecto!

Ingredients

- 1 lbs. wild-caught shrimp
- 1 can diced tomatoes, 14oz
- 1 can tomato paste, 6oz
- 2 small onions, diced
- 1 cup vegetable broth
- 2 tsp. garlic, minced
- 1 tbsp. Italian parsley
- 1 tsp. oregano
- 1 tsp. basil
- 1/2 tsp. thyme
- 1 tsp. sea salt
- 1/2 tsp. pepper
- 1 bay leaf

Directions

1. Add all ingredients except shrimp.
2. Mix to ensure an even coating.
3. Cook on low for 3 hours.
4. Add shrimp and cook for 25 more minutes (make sure shrimp is pink).
5. Discard bay leaf before eating.

Shoal to Shore Clam Chowder

This soup captures and retains all the essence of a beachside clam dig without the hassle of shucking, chopping, and cleaning. For the freshest taste, start with canned clams containing no other added ingredients besides salt and water.

Ingredients

- 2 cans clams, chopped
- 1 cup carrots, diced
- 2 medium onions, chopped
- 1/2 cup celery, chopped
- 2 cups tomato juice
- 1 cup free range chicken broth
- 1/2 cup tomato paste
- 1 tbsp. parsley
- 2 tsp. oregano
- 1 tsp. thyme
- 1 tsp. garlic
- 1/2 tsp. crushed red pepper
- 1 tsp. sea salt
- 1/4 tsp. black pepper

Directions

1. Add all ingredients to crock pot.
2. Mix to ensure an even coating.
3. Cook on low for 8 hours.

Lucky Native Turkey Soup

Early Americans must have felt fortunate indeed when they managed to trap a wild turkey. The dark, nutty meat with intense woody flavors holds up well to long roasting over a fire - or to long hours simmering in a crock pot. Serve this dish with primitive classic-sweet potatoes to make an unforgettable impression any time!

Ingredients

- 2 lbs. skinless boneless turkey breasts, cut into chunks
- 2 cups free range chicken broth
- 3/4 cup coconut milk (full-fat)
- 3 sweet potatoes, chopped
- 1 cup carrots, chopped
- 2 small onions, chopped
- 1/2 cup celery, chopped
- 2 tbsp. extra virgin olive oil
- 1 tsp. sea salt
- 1/2 pepper
- 1 bay leaf
- 2 tsp. dill
- 1/2 tbsp. arrowroot

Directions

1. Add all ingredients (except arrowroot) to crock pot.
2. Mix to ensure an even coating.
3. Cook on low for 7 hours.
4. Add arrowroot after cooking. Stir and leave uncovered. Let thicken for 20 minutes.

5   Discard bay leaf before serving.

Primordial Herb Pot Turkey

We're pulling out all the stops to make this sweet and savory turkey breast memorable. Loads of garlic enhance (but don't overwhelm) the rich natural flavor of the fowl. Basil, honey, and mustard provide an unexpected, tingly twist.

Ingredients

- 3 lbs. turkey breast, bone-in
- 1/2 cup free range chicken broth
- 2 tbsp. mustard
- 1 tbsp. raw honey
- 2 tsp. garlic, minced
- 1 tsp. thyme
- 1 tsp. basil
- 1 tsp. sea salt
- 1/4 tsp. pepper
- 1 tsp. rosemary

Directions

1. Mix all dry ingredients: garlic, honey, and mustard.
2. Rub into dry turkey and place turkey in middle of crock pot.
3. Add chicken broth.
4. Cook on low for 7 hours.

Thanksgiving Forever Sweet Potatoes

If you think the high point of every holiday table is the sweet potato "side", you're going to love this recipe. And, why wait for Thanksgiving anyway? Serve this nutritious, pecan and apple-laced sweet with any meal.

Ingredients

- 6 sweet potatoes, chopped into chunks
- 2 apples, peeled, cored, chopped into chunks
- 2 tbsp. raw honey
- 2 tbsp. ghee
- 2 tsp. ground cinnamon
- 1/4 tsp. ginger
- 1/4 tsp. nutmeg
- 1/2 cup pecans, chopped
- 1/2 tsp. vanilla extract

Directions

1. Add all ingredients to crock pot (except pecans).
2. Gently mix all ingredients.
3. Cook on low for 7 hours.
4. Garnish with pecans before serving.

Bursting with Basil Chicken Minestrone

Out with the beans, pasta, and rice; in with the mushrooms when the original Italian vegetable soup gets our Paleo makeover. In point of fact, most "shrooms" add deep flavor to any liquid. What kind of mushrooms you choose to use is up to you. Crimini are always a good option, but white button mushrooms are closely related both in taste and texture. If you want to "kick it up a notch" try adding a handful of dried wild mushrooms as well.

Ingredients

- 2 lbs. skinless boneless free range chicken breast, chopped
- 4 cups free range chicken broth
- 1 can tomato paste (6oz)
- 1/2 cup carrots, diced
- 1/2 cup celery, diced
- 2 medium onions, chopped
- 1 package of mushrooms
- 2 tsp. garlic minced
- 1 can diced tomatoes
- 1 tbsp. basil
- 1 tsp. oregano
- 1 tsp. sea salt
- 1/2 tsp. pepper

Directions

1. Add all ingredients to crock pot.
2. Gently mix all ingredients.
3. Cook on low for 7 hours.

Vegetable Stew

Leeks are at the heart of this dish, just as they were in many stone age meals. Like a mild cross between an onion and garlic, if you haven't cooked with leeks before, you're in for a treat. The ultimate "earthy" food they really do grow wild (now often domesticated) in marshy areas, so be sure to clean between the layers to rinse out any residual mud. The body and texture they lend this soup makes it well worth the effort!

Ingredients

- 2 cups carrots, chopped
- 1 cup parsnips, chopped
- 1 medium onion, sliced
- 1/2 cup celery, chopped
- 1/2 cup leeks, sliced
- 2 cups vegetable broth
- 1 can diced tomatoes, 14oz
- 1 package baby bella mushrooms
- 2 tsp. garlic, minced
- 2 tbsp. extra virgin olive oil
- 1 tsp. thyme
- 1 tsp. rosemary
- 1/4 tsp. oregano
- 1 tsp. sea salt
- 1/4 tsp. pepper
- 1/2 tbsp. arrowroot

Directions

1. Add all ingredients to crock pot (except arrowroot).

2   Gently mix all ingredients.

3   Cook on low for 7 hours.

4   Add arrowroot after cooking. Stir and leave uncovered. Let thicken for 20 minutes.

Dessert

Day at the Country Fair Caramelized Apples

Saving the best for last, dessert! This caramel apple treat eliminates processed sugar without sacrificing gooey goodness. In fact, the slow cook method actually drives the honey and raisin essence deep into the fruit instead of merely coating it. You get all the sweet flavor of candied apples without the stick!

Ingredients

- 5 Granny Smith apples, cored, sliced
- 3 tbsp. raw honey
- 1 tbsp. cinnamon
- 1/2 cup raisins
- 1/4 cup walnuts, diced
- 4 tbsp. Ghee
- 1/2 tsp. nutmeg
- 1/4 tsp. ginger

Directions

1. Add all ingredients to crock pot.
2. Gently mix all ingredients.
3. Cook on low for 3 hours.

Printed in Great Britain
by Amazon